Go for It...

Mastering Negotiations

Go for It...

Mastering Negotiations

WIN WIN

Sharon M. Weinstein

Stephen Weinstein

Go for It... Mastering Negotiations

Cover Design by Kimb Williams

Printed in the United States of America

ISBN-10: 0-9989384-0-8

ISBN-13: 978-0-9989384-0-0

Available from Amazon.com and other online stores

For information about this title or to order additional books, contact the publisher: SMWGroup LLC, Visit the website at:

http:/smwgroupllc.com

or call 1.202.798.0092

info@smwgroupllc.com

Dedication

Negotiations are a fact of life... they occur at every level from home to work, from childhood to adulthood. When we are open to learning, we can learn the most from those nearest and dearest to us... our children!

Go for It... Mastering Negotiations
is dedicated to our children.

We have learned from them.

TABLE OF CONTENTS

INTRODUCTION

Masters at negotiation, the authors share their years of firsthand experience in negotiating for the all-win outcome. Sharon learned negotiations with Ministers of Health and Education in countries throughout Eastern Europe, and C-Suite leaders worldwide. In negotiating strategy that would benefit all parties, she mastered the fine art of negotiating for leadership and keeping her cool under pressure. Stephen, a hospital turnaround specialist, learned the art of the deal by making financially-compromised hospitals' cash-flow profitable. With limited resources, and without compromising quality, he turned failures into successes.

An understanding of both sides of the aisle or ocean is essential to one's negotiating and leadership success. Agreements and relationships are critical in today's global business environment. In this book, you will gain the negotiation strategies needed to handle difficult people, manage conflict, and pick your battles. Preparation is the key to feeling both confident and ready to create an all-win outcome. In this tell-all approach to negotiations, the reader will learn how voice, body language, eye contact, and, yes, personality, affect behaviors, outcomes, and communication. From Main Street to Wall Street, *Go for It* engages the reader in mastering the negotiation.

ACKNOWLEDGEMENTS

The authors acknowledge the contributions by Heidi Weinstein-Levy, Jason M. Weinstein, and Dr. Marla Vannucci.

These three brilliant negotiators bring a wealth of experience to the table; individually, they have negotiated employment packages, benefits, academic appointments, and criminal and civil cases.

They understand human behavior and the goal of an all-win outcome!

CHAPTER 1
NEGOTIATION 101

EACH OF US

We are all negotiators — every day of our lives. The term "101" is consistent with the basics, and a natural starting point, regardless of skill level.

What is negotiation? A practical definition could be: "Negotiation is being able to make the other person an offer or proposal that they would find more attractive than their next-best alternative, or something they cannot refuse."

Some consider negotiation the art of deal-making. It is certainly that; it is sharing with others the merits of your offer or proposal. Negotiation is nothing more than communication with different starting positions. Knowing what those posts are, and understanding the people who hold them as opposed to making assumptions about who they are, is how we get to a good resolution. A mutually-beneficial resolution is our goal!

To negotiate successfully, we must *begin with the end in mind*. Start with a plan! The process is simple, but each step is critical to the outcome.

1. Know the why.

2. Be prepared.

3. Follow the tips and understand the rationale.

4. Know your common ground.

5. Open with your case: this demonstrates confidence.

6. Listen actively.

7. Support your case with facts.

8. Explore agreement and disagreement, and understand the possibilities.

9. Indicate your readiness to work together.

10. Know your options.

11. Advance to closure by confirming the details.

12. Make it happen.

CONSIDER THESE TIPS AND RATIONALE

Tip	Rationale
Know what you are willing to accept and be honest about your requirements.	You will be empowered in support of your interests. Your listener will recognize your confidence level.
Do not disclose what you are willing to accept in terms of salary or conditions. Have a deal-breaker in mind, e.g., lack of flexibility in hours.	This will compromise your negotiating power.
Determine what the other party is willing to accept.	It is better to know the alternatives up front than to second-guess.
Be an active listener, like a student.	Assume there are things about the situation that you don't understand. Let the other party know that you have heard and understood what has been said.

Whether it is a business or personal negotiation, you must have a goal! Let's begin with the most basic transaction.

LET'S BUY A CAR

We have each, at one time or another, purchased an automobile. Maybe, like an informed healthcare consumer, you have searched the web, you know the value of the car you want, you have checked the apps online that share the current value — and you are prepared for the encounter with the new or used-car salesperson.

Historically, car dealers take a bad ride — no pun intended. Let's face it; their reputations are not stellar. The consumer often thinks that they are being taken advantage of and that they will leave — with or without the car — an unhappy camper.

You see the 'come-on' ad in the newspaper or on TV; of course, the car offered at that fantastic price is the basic model. If you want heated seats, navigation, parking assistance and more — you will pay more for the 'options.' Yes, it does seem as if everything and anything is a possible option. The model that you saw on the showroom floor is loaded with options, and the car that you take for a test drive may also be loaded with options. You level with the salesman, sharing what you must have, as well as what you would like to have, and he or she offers a price. Of course, the price is much more than you intended to spend, even though you initially shared a budget.

You strategically change your list; perhaps those must-haves are not as essential after all, and perhaps you can settle. Again, you are offered a price, and again, the sales person will discuss it with the financial manager to ensure that the price is 'final' and the 'best that they can do.' After all, they are barely making a penny on the sale!

You are not the new kid on the block. You have been buying cars since before Joe Salesman was born. You have been around the block, and more importantly, you are not afraid to walk away from the offer and the deal.

What did the salesman fail to do?

- Listen
- Communicate
- Be honest
- Trust
- Respect
- Understand
- Affirm
- Believe

The salesman made multiple mistakes, beginning with a misunderstanding of basic negotiations.

A SICK DAY WITH AN UN-SICK CHILD

Tyler doesn't feel well today, or so he says. Is it because he was up all-night vomiting, did not get sufficient sleep, or because there is a test today and he is unprepared? Know the facts, the goals, and the results that will represent an all-win. Maybe he will stay home!

Start with *WHY?* Why does he think that he is sick? Was he vomiting? Is he feverish or sleep-deprived? Did he finish his homework or not? Most kids are not as sophisticated as Ferris Bueller, who really worked his parents to get a day off. Some kids fake being sick because they're tired of homework; some kids fake being sick because they're bullied; and sometimes, kids just need a break, just like adults.

How do you know the truth? You come to the negotiation prepared with the following action plan:

- Check temperature
- Ask about symptoms
- Listen, look, and feel for signs of vomiting

You get the picture. And we'll elaborate on it later in Chapter 5 when we discuss relationships.

These are just two examples of negotiation at the basic level — level 101 — and where you will begin!

Before you proceed, you must first have a sense of self. You must explore why we are all different, and what those differences mean when we are collaborating, implementing, and negotiating.

Let's examine what makes us unique.

Chapter 2

Self-Awareness

WE ARE DIFFERENT

We are all different; our styles differ, our personalities differ, and our outcomes differ. Each of us gets from point A to point B in our own way. Our upbringing, education, mindset, attitude, and, yes, our personalities, have a direct effect on our outcomes. People negotiate differently and behave differently during the negotiation process.

Our differences can be better understood by applying the Myers-Briggs Type Indicator (MBTI). MBTI is a series of questions based on psychology. By responding to the questions, people can learn about the choices they make and their worldviews. By answering the MBTI questions, people are placed into one of sixteen groups. There are no rights or wrongs here, in either answering the questions or to which group we're assigned; each of us brings different skill sets and gifts to the table and each of us of has value in our own way.

THE EIGHT LETTERS

How do we get from eight letters to 16 personality types? Each type has four different letters, generating a total of 16 personality types. Although you may lean in a direction, you may also be a combination of types. Let's examine what each letter represents.

You have heard the terms *extrovert* and *introvert*. Perhaps you think of yourself as an *extrovert* (E), more outgoing at social events, getting your energies from others. Or, maybe you consider yourself an *introvert* (I), gaining strength from within. Again, one is not better than the other.

Also, *extroverts* are not always loud, and *introverts* are not always quiet. *Introverts* may enjoy social gatherings, and *extroverts* sometimes need downtime. Let's look more closely:

Extrovert (E)	Introvert (I)
Gains energy from others	Gains energy from within
Speaks for clarification	Thinks for clarification
Seen as easy to know	Seen as difficult to get to know
Works well with others	Works well alone
Has varied relationships	Has few close relationships
Interaction	Concentration
Makes decisions quickly	Self-reflective

Let's examine *intuitive* (N) and *sensing* (S). In this case, the letters express how we consume information. Those who are *intuitive* take in information and understand it through patterns, impressions, and possibilities — while those who are *sensing* use their five senses and facts.

Intuitive (N)	Sensing (S)
Process through patterns	Process through the five senses
Futuristic	Thinks in the present
Abstract thinker	Concrete thinker
Sees a bigger picture	Notices the details
Idealistic	Practical
Theoretical	Fact-based
Gathers information from underlying patterns	Collects information from what they see, touch, feel

Now, let's switch gears to *feeling* (F) and *thinking* (T). Do you make decisions based on feelings and values, or on facts? Do you use your heart or your head in the decision-making process? Everyone will have traits of both in different situations; this is about your inclination and not about an absolute!

Feeling (F)	Thinking (T)
Decides with the heart	Concludes with the head
Feelings-based	Logic-based
Driven by emotion	Powered by fact/thought
Empathic	Critical
Prioritizes relationships	Prioritizes truth
Personalizes remarks	Not easily upset by remarks
Passionate	Rational
Personal	Impersonal

What are the final two letters? They are *perceiving* (P) and *judging* (J), and they are about preference! *Perceivers* prefer an open-ended world and are sometimes more spontaneous. *Judgers* prefer more structure and control.

Perceiving (P)	Judging (J)
Many incomplete irons in the fire	Prefers to finish one thing before beginning another
Options remain open	Moves toward closure
Flexible	Structured
Spontaneous	Plans before doing
Less organized	More organized
Relaxed	Controlling
May procrastinate	Responsible and decisive
May change midway	Sticks to the plan

Use the descriptions above and the diagrams below to identify the keys to your personality.

Extroverts (energized by people, multitaskers)

Sensors (realists who focus on details and common sense)

Introverts (like working in small groups, focus on one thing at a time)

Intuitives (focus on the big picture and value innovation)

Thinkers (logical consistent, fair, honest)

Judgers (organized and prepared, follow rules)

Feelers (sensitive and cooperative)

Perceivers (keep options open, act spontaneously, are flexible)

What, and who, are you?

In a former position, our entire workforce was required to take Myers-Briggs to determine personality styles and to acknowledge who would make a good workgroup partner. Our results were posted on our office or cubicle doors to facilitate workflow and planning.

THE OUTCOMES

Although it is an unusual result, I came up an even 25% in each of the four categories and could get along with anyone and complete any job on time. My husband varied his responses and thus his outcomes — testing the test and his personal style. He, too, could work with anyone — as a result of manipulating the responses based on the time and day of the week.

His approach was unintentional — or was it?

Why MBTI and what will you glean from the experience?

1. When used correctly, you will understand all types.
2. You know that you are not alone.
3. You have an objective way of viewing co-workers.
4. You understand the energy cycle.
5. You can use your preferences to find your strengths.

Now that we know who we are, we can discover how *behavior, appearance, voice, and body language affect negotiations.*

Chapter 3

Optimizing Style

BEHAVIOR / APPEARANCE

How we act, what we say, and our body language — these factors affect our ability to be heard, to communicate, and to negotiate. People skills can make the difference between the win, lose, and all-win!

Let's begin with behavior

Attitude can and will affect outcomes. Your counterpart can and will observe your behavior and make assumptions based upon perception. Think about the election process in your country and what the actions of the candidates during debate tell you about the person.

What can you do to enhance awareness of and commitment to the best negotiating habits?

1. Be aware of your attitude.
2. Listen to the other party; concentrate on active listening and a complete awareness of what he or she is saying. After all, you have two ears and a single mouth.
3. Be patient; patience sometimes frustrates the other party who is eager to move on.
4. Be focused on the outcome; satisfaction for the other party equates to feeling fulfilled, whether or not it was what he wanted.
5. Think, "If you, then I..." In a two-party negotiation, each party must be willing to make concessions.
6. Don't be afraid to walk away; know your BATNA (see Chapter 7).

Appearance

As speakers or those addressing audiences, we assess the type of audience; we ask questions to familiarize ourselves with the setting, the normal attire, and the venue. As negotiators, we do the same. We want to be familiar with the style, the attire, the mood, the location. Remember that first impressions count!

NOW, WE TURN TO VOICE

You hear parents tell their children to, "Use your words." As adults, do we 'use our own words?' Think before you speak and choose relevant words. Think about your tone, quality, dialect, grammar, and purpose. Modulate and change the tempo, volume, and emphasis. Pause as needed, and paraphrase to ensure understanding. Breathe from your lower abdomen.

Avoid the following:

- Foul language
- Rudeness or disrespectful tone
- Stammering
- Hesitation
- Argumentation

FINALLY, BODY LANGUAGE

What is your body language revealing about you; what are you telling your audience? View the body in four quadrants:

Quadrant	Response
Face and head	The doorway to the heart and soul
Body	Leaning-in, positioning, stance, posture
Hands	Voluntary (confident) or involuntary (lack of confidence) movements
Legs	Uncrossed (denotes trustworthiness); feet flat on floor (positive signal)

Body language is a critical business tool. Now that you are familiar with the quadrants, let's put them to use with these body-language tips:

Action	Why
Nod your head	Creates alignment by maintaining eye contact; defuses tension
Mirror the action	Suggests engagement by adopting the other person's behavior – lean-in, lean-out and more
Mind your hands	Exudes confidence by placing hands just below your chest with fingers together
Mind your feet	Shows resolve by planting them firmly on the floor
Relax the body and assume an open posture	Builds trust
Smile	Demonstrates calm confidence
Maintain eye contact	Shows engagement

Style has been mastered, and we are ready, with calm confidence, *to explore the role of stress and negotiations*

CHAPTER 4

STRESS AND NEGOTIATIONS

Stress plays a significant role in our ability to be well, stay well, and function within our busy lives. It can also affect our capacity to negotiate for such things as workplace balance. One of the greatest stressors we face is the need to negotiate within the workplace. Let's consider *balance*.

NEGOTIATING FOR WORKPLACE BALANCE

Tired — overworked — emotionally and physically drained? Are your aging parents challenged, or is your young child ill? Are you a part of that sandwich generation — caught between aging parents and teenagers? Is your partner out of work, or overworked? If any of these scenarios describe you, you are a candidate for *balance*. If you know your skills, abilities, and performance record are secure and valued, you have a solid footing for negotiating flexible work arrangements.

"Life is like riding a bike. It is impossible to maintain your balance while standing still."

— Linda Brakeall

In *B is for Balance: 12 Steps Toward a More Balanced Life at Home and at Work*, the author (Sharon Weinstein) tells us that good employers recognize the value of good employees, and they are often willing and able to find or create ways to help current employees deal with short-term or permanent changes caused by family situations. The changes can include flextime, job-sharing, telecommuting, or part-time employment.

You may think that it is impossible within your work environment, but you may be pleasantly surprised. You won't know until you address the issue!

Negotiation is a critical component of creating workplace balance and it is fundamental in avoiding workplace burnout.

BURNOUT

If you are a busy person with a demanding job and family and friends who seek your attention, you are blessed — but only if you can handle it. If you are an entrepreneur, or if you work from your home, that can be an additional benefit because you can have some control over your schedule and integrate your job and personal life. If you travel extensively for business, however, you may feel your own time slipping away. You may be experiencing burnout! Remember that some of the busiest people feel guilty regardless of what they are doing. Is that you?

We can prevent burnout by following the advice of experts and those who have been there themselves. The main point they make is that we benefit greatly from maintaining clear boundaries between our work lives and our personal lives.

Think of ways in which you can prevent burnout in your work environment:

1)
_____

2)
_____

3)
_____

4)
_____

5)
_____

ESTABLISHING CLEAR BOUNDARIES

When your work and personal life blend under the guise of 'multitasking,' then both the work and your personal life suffer. When you are at work, focus on the job to be done. When you are finished with work, don't bring it home with you — make time for your personal life. If your work materials are dispersed throughout nearly every room of your house, then you have no place for a real retreat. If you're always talking on the cell phone or checking your email while you're with a friend or family member, your time with that person is not of high quality. Take a chance to focus exclusively on that person for a while. Then you will remember that experience when you're working, and you won't feel guilty that you must concentrate on work. Create high-quality work and personal experiences for yourself by keeping them separate.

Create a designated work area at home

When you are in your home office, prepare your presentations, review your contracts, pay your invoices, and focus on paper and electronic mail to be answered and other work to be done. When you have finished that work, leave the office and the computer. Instead of always checking email throughout the day, set aside specific time intervals and do it then.

Then, reward yourself with personal time.

Become an efficiency expert

Many professionals who work from home find the adjustment difficult. The freedom of working in casual clothing, of not reporting for work at a given time, of not being directly supervised by others — creates an environment that may become lax. You must be responsible for your efficiency, effectiveness, and efforts. Is your work environment efficient and ergonomically correct? Does it lend to a high level of productivity in a short timespan? Are you a morning person and do you do your best work in the early hours of the day? Use the same schedule to plan your work at home, and then work your plan.

Schedule time for meals, relaxation, and exercise

You schedule multiple appointments in your planner. Schedule time with *yourself*. Make appointments for regular exercise, a hearty walk, meditation, or other leisure activities.

If you find that you don't have the discipline to keep the appointment with yourself, find a friend or family member you can include in the healthy activity, and make an appointment with them. It will be harder to postpone, and you'll have the bonus of quality time with that person. Negotiate on behalf of yourself!

Know what is important

In the book *the 7 Habits of Highly Effective People*, Stephen Covey showed that for many of us, the day is filled with tasks that seem urgent but are not important. Those activities attract our attention, but it is possible that they may never need to be done. Weed those out, and make time for the important tasks. The essential duties that are also urgent require our immediate attention.

Recognize the need for help

You are not alone. Some people can help you. Share your feelings with friends and family, and let them pick up the ball for you when you need help. In turn, make it a practice to be of service to others and to pay it forward. Many people say that when they feel stressed out, if they go out of their way to help someone else, they feel better afterward. Pay it forward, and change the world one good deed at a time.

Know thyself

Are you an assertive type who finds it easy to say no? Or are you the selfless type who takes on more than you can handle? Negotiate for workplace balance by knowing thyself and thy limitations.

Have the right people in the right seats on the bus!

In Jim C. Collins' classic book *Good to Great: Why Some Companies Make the Leap... and Others Don't*, the author alludes to having the right people in the right seats on the bus. It is not enough to have lots of help if the help is not the right support for the right job. Make a concerted effort to surround yourself with good people, and give them the latitude they need to do a good job.

Tend to your own interests

Winston Churchill said that a laborer benefits from physical rest and a sedentary person benefits from exercise. As Churchill put it, "One cannot mend the frayed elbows of a coat by rubbing the sleeves or shoulders; but the tired parts of the mind can be rested and strengthened, not merely by rest, but by using other parts. It is not enough simply to switch off the lights which play upon the main and ordinary field of interest; a new field of interest must be illuminated."

Try something new

You may know that what you are doing now is not working for you. Perhaps the balance between work and personal life is out of gear. Working harder at the same activities does not create balance; sometimes, it is better to switch gears and move full speed ahead.

Change your schedule or alter your routine. Exercise in the morning instead of after work. Find a combination that works best for you and that re-energizes your life. Don't keep doing the exact thing or trying to compact more of the same in less amount of time expecting a different result.

It just won't work!

Family-friendly work environments

Family-Friendly Working and Work-Life Balance refer to working arrangements that facilitate the achievement of a better balance between professional and family life. These may include maternity/paternity leave, on-site child care, flextime, job-sharing, work-from-home, and other creative solutions to workplace balance.

If you have some priorities in life regarding flexible working or part-time employment, it is good to inform of your expectations during the interview process. You may otherwise end up in a position in which you are dissatisfied with the working conditions and not able to handle the stress at work together with managing your family. Job-hopping can be stressful and may not be possible at all when the economy is a challenge.

Re-entering the workforce

If you are re-entering the workforce after taking time off to be at home to look after your kids or for other personal reasons, you may be considering only a part-time work schedule or flexible timings. Ideally, plans should be addressed during the interview process.

Demonstrate the value that you bring to the workforce by having balance in your home life.

If your goal is to work part-time, consider the following:

- How many hours can you work without benefits?
- Would your manager be supportive of the situation?
- If not, could you be more flexible?

Negotiating to switch from full to part-time

Ideally, switching from full to part-time should not be a challenge and can easily be negotiated. You may, however, consider working from home so many hours a day to demonstrate your credibility and efficiency. As discussions continue, your track record of excellence could work in your favor.

Negotiate based on a project. If your current assignment requires skill sets that only you can provide, negotiate your time and availability accordingly. Be flexible in continuing on a full-time basis until the project is underway; then, negotiate a part-time schedule in your favor.

CONFLICT

Conflict is a fact of life; it occurs at home and work. Most conflict can be addressed between parties. Long-standing conflict can affect performance, corporate culture, and retention. The ability to recognize and understand conflict, and bring timely resolution, will serve you and your staff well.

Rules for Those in Conflict	Actions
Both parties agree to resolve the dispute in a respectful way	After cool-down period, arrange for both sides to meet at a neutral location
Listen carefully and be honest	All parties describe conflict in clear terms, including behaviors,

	feelings, and desired outcomes
Take responsibility for behavior	Focus on the problem, not the people
Be willing to compromise	Restate and summarize Brainstorm solutions and listen to options Summarize Shake hands and agree to action

Work-life balance

We all have responsibilities, whether it is caring for children and elderly parents or the pursuit of personal interests, activities, or hobbies. Balance is the responsibility of employer and employee. Today's companies are always seeking ways to assist their workers in managing their job responsibilities along with their family and personal responsibilities and needs outside of work.

They are willing to negotiate — are you?

Stress has an impact on *relationships* — in employment, with family, during travel, and in multicultural situations.

CHAPTER 5

RELATIONSHIPS

WORK

Work is an ongoing negotiation — regardless of the work setting and your position within the organization. We just addressed the stressors associated with the workplace.

Examples might include staff negotiations related to hours, compensation, benefits, bonus targets and payouts, outcomes, expectations, performance, or co-workers. It might involve revenue-generation, cost-cutting or margin-optimization, customer/client service issues or service recovery/customer service. Anything and everything involves the art of negotiation.

THE JOB... THE ULTIMATE NEGOTIATION

Compensation

Remember that the organization needs you as much as you need the job. There is always a dearth of talented people. A team is always trying to attract the 'right fit' talent, and if you have the caliber and skills and can demonstrate that to the organization, you will be financially rewarded. If you have reached the salary-negotiation round in the recruiting cycle, which in all probable cases is the last round, the hiring team believes you are a strong fit for the role. If negotiating face-to-face, sit straight, be confident, and make eye contact with the other party. Be well-groomed, including hair and nails. Dress appropriately.

If the negotiation is over the telephone, follow the same rule of thumb. Be professional.

What can and what should you do?

Go well prepared before the salary-negotiation round. Do your research ahead of time. Determine the current market trend and see if you can learn about the company's compensation philosophy and structure. Identify the market rate for the role based on competitive market data. Be honest about your current salary. Some organizations do verify salary. Consider what you want and why!

- What do you enjoy most/least about your current position?

- What do you like/dislike about your employer?
- What would you seek in a new employer?
- What is your *WHY* surrounding your career trajectory?
- Why would you consider a new role/relocation?
- Where do you see yourself in five years?
- What is the opportunity for advancement now?
- Have you had a counter-offer; if so, how did you handle it?

Remember that you shouldn't negotiate during the offer conversation. That suggests you're asking for more money, without stopping to think twice about what they're offering you — both the intangibles and the tangible.

Take time to reflect on their offer. Most companies will allow you time to review their offer anyway. Use this time to scrutinize every inch of the compensation package — from the base salary, all the way to the benefits and incentives.

Be respectful, not desperate; it shows every time. If you want to make a counter-offer, be prepared to offer an intellectual rationale for why you deserve more than is offered.

Regional salaries or salaries comparable to other companies may not apply to your unique skillset. Differentiate yourself from others in the same arena, re salary. If agreement cannot be made, and the negotiations fail, know that you are willing to walk away gracefully.

To summarize, consider these key points:

- Be reasonable in your request
- Demonstrate your value/worth
- Understand the company's compensation philosophy
- Know the decision-makers
- Recognize that money is not the only thing that matters; be aware of what else you want

Look at the last bullet point. Yes, there is more to compensation than salary. Let's talk packages.

You got the job offer, but the salary is a little low. Do you counter? Surprisingly, many people don't.

Nearly three in 5 U.S. employees accepted the salary they were initially offered at their most recent or current job and did not negotiate, according to a Glassdoor Salary Negotiation Insights Survey released in May 2016. What's more, women are less likely to negotiate than men. Almost 7 in 10 female respondents — 68% — did not negotiate salary versus 52% of the male respondents.

If we don't advocate for ourselves, who will? Before accepting a job, check out these tips to negotiate your best compensation package and to position yourself for long-term financial success.

Know your numbers

"Compensation varies widely, so compare pay levels to those that have similar job titles and functions and are in your geographic location," advises Dan Ryan, a principal at executive search firm Ryan Search & Consulting and a member of the Special Expertise panel for the Society for Human Resource Management. Here are some sources for this type of information:

- Payscale.com
- Glassdoor.com
- Salary.com
- Bureau of Labor Statistics' free wage data
- American Society of Civil Engineers
- Other associations

Incentive plans

"For entry to mid-level candidates, ask about a hiring bonus, a performance review after six months, or even a larger workspace," Ryan says. Be flexible on how the compensation package is bundled. In exchange for a more robust health care plan or a flexible work schedule, consider accepting a lower base salary. "Every candidate has specific needs, and there is almost always an opportunity for candidates and firms to negotiate in these areas," Ryan says.

Take the time to consider what you are paying now for benefits. Subtract that number from your On-Target Compensation (OTC) to get a sense of our actual net earnings. Do the same for the company's offer — they may be offering you a lower salary than you want but the benefit costs are less, so you may be netting out more than you think.

Paid-leave benefits demonstrate a focus on balance. High prices are the greatest barrier to providing paid leave; family-leave benefit can be a differentiator in today's competitive talent marketplace. Family dynamics are changing due to our largest living generations, including Millennials and Baby Boomers.

Salary or bonus...that is the question

And, the answer is, "It all depends." You cannot generalize because it depends on the company and its compensation philosophy. For example, a company might target base salaries at the median of the market and put more leverage on its variable components (and equity, if applicable) to increase the competitiveness of the offer. For most mid-level corporate roles, we see a higher focus on base versus bonus. Some roles might not even be bonus-eligible. In the consulting world, we typically see more leverage put on the variable and equity components, which resembles a more pay-for-performance strategy. When you are negotiating an offer, you are negotiating base and what is known as a target bonus. In some companies, based upon performance, you can exceed the target. If a company does not perform well, it won't pay out at the target. Losses impact outcome.

Are bonuses guaranteed? Rarely! In most organizations, bonus payouts are based on both company and individual performance. If you performed well, but your firm did not meet its targets, that will have an impact on your actual bonus payout. You cannot expect a full bonus in that circumstance. Conversely, if the company performed well and you received a high-performance rating, you might see a bonus payout that exceeds your bonus target.

If you are asked to sign a Non-Disclosure Agreement (NDA), make sure the employer understands that anything you already know doesn't apply. You must map this out.

If you sign a non-compete agreement, be aware of the length of time and geographical distance from the place of employment.

Benefits might include:

- ➡ Child and Elder care: find out what the employer offers regarding payment or referrals

- ➡ Compensation or Flex time: for every extra hour you work overtime, you can take an hour off (the system may require you to keep accurate records)

- ➡ Family-friendly: look for work-life balance (see Chapter 4)

- ➡ Insurance: this may include life and disability

- ➡ Professional development: look for budgeted funds for your professional growth
- ➡ Tuition reimbursement: this may be possible

The recruiter has a job to do. He or she will identify the type of candidate you are (active or passive) and ask the questions that will qualify or disqualify you from consideration. The recruiter may ask if anything is going on in your current situation that would prevent you from making a move today. The responses might include the ability to remain local or to relocate after completing the sale of your home.

Perhaps you are expecting an upcoming bonus payout, and you want to remain with your current employer until you receive the bonus. Recruiters are strategic, and you must also be strategic. They want to establish a healthy relationship with the candidate; it is an art — not a science! They do so by building a strong relationship with the candidate, asking the right questions, and knowing how to get to *yes*.

They are looking for someone closable; when the answers do not match, or the candidate cannot start for six months, they need to reconsider whether they can make the negotiation work. In each interaction with you, they are learning more and more about you, and they know that if there is not a match — they must walk away.

Sign-on bonuses

We talked about bonuses in general as they relate to the company and individual performance.

Let's talk sign-on bonuses.

They are sometimes used by companies to close possible gaps in the offer package; if the company's offer is short $5-10,000 and it cannot give more, it may offer a sign-on bonus. If they are working against a competitive offer and have matched the competitive offer, but they want to increase the competitiveness of their offer, they may offer a sign-on bonus.

If your new employers want and need you to begin immediately, but a possible bonus payout at the existing employer is on the table, they may have you start earlier and make you whole. Note that almost all companies have a claw-back — meaning that if they offer you a sign-on, and you leave before 12 months of employment, you are liable for repaying that sign-on bonus. The sign-on may also be incremental, rather than a pre-employment bonus.

Relocating... it will eventually happen

Sooner or later, you might take a job that will require you and your family to move. You may incur significant expenses in the process, and if you are like most people, you will want your employer to pay for a portion of those costs, especially with changes in the tax laws. How do you handle negotiations related to relocation?

Some companies have a standard relocation policy; you may be able to negotiate more. Other companies handle relocation on a case-by-case basis.

What is your company's policy?

Examples of expenses may or may not include the following:

- Pack your goods with a national mover, load/transport
- One vehicle is included
- Pay for two weeks of temporary housing/rental car
- Cover up to one month of storage
- If needed, ask for more temp housing up to a given amount
- Relief in housing, not selling or buying
- Help with finding a new place

A negotiation about relocation compensation is the same as any other negotiation. If you focus on adequate preparation, collaborative negotiating, and out-of-the-box thinking, you will do well.

Focus on your interests

The whole point of negotiating for something is to address your real needs. Before you limit your expectations, make sure you know what you want. The bottom line is that you need the bottom line.

Don't take the job if you need a second job to make your budget.

Get it in writing

Once you and the company agree on a compensation package for your relocation expenses, make sure you capture that agreement in writing. A formal contract may or may not be necessary. Sometimes a simple signed letter will do, detailing the assistance that is being provided and by what time. In most companies, it is standard to provide an offer letter (via email or regular mail), and that document will require your signature to confirm your acceptance.

THE NON-EMPLOYEE

We are not all employees; it is essential to consider the contracted staff member or independent agent.

Physician recruitment to grow volume

Within the healthcare setting, physicians may or may not be employees but they do affect profitability. More physicians mean more patients, and more patients mean more income. Let's discuss physician recruitment to grow specialty practice within a hospital and the bottom line. In a Texas-based community hospital, we offered medical-surgical services. We outsourced specialty services, including eye, skin, bone, and women's health to other facilities. We lost potential revenue on those services, and we also lost patients. Our reputation was that of a general hospital — one that could offer only the basics — and thus was less than full-service.

A patient in need of a knee replacement traveled more than 30 miles south to see a specialty board-certified physician. It made perfect sense to bring that medical practitioner, and orthopedic services, to our community setting. By researching start-up orthopedic practices, we located a young physician who was eager to expand his outreach by traveling 30 miles north one day weekly to grow an extended practice. The doctor would provide his staff, and we would offer location and referrals.

His practice grew substantially and established a template for future development of specialty practices within our more remote setting. Our hospital was soon at capacity occupancy; we had a waiting list for elective cases, and a reputation as a quality, full-service provider. We had previously been dependent on county funds; with our newfound return on investment, dollars previously earmarked for us were now a part of the school budget.

Finances drive initiatives

In another facility in the Midwest, as Chief Executive Officer of a 200-bed hospital with only 50 occupied beds, we were in a financial bind. To increase the census, and the bottom line, we recruited a five-physician practice with 20 admissions in a neighboring hospital. By bringing their physicians to our facility, we gained their patients and a new revenue stream. They owned their two-story building, fully equipped. In return for purchasing their building at a fee of $1.5 million, they agreed to bring their patients to us. By negotiating strategically, we settled on a mere $1 million price tag — in return for which we offered them a deluxe wing of the hospital and a complete nursing staff. They benefitted by seeing their patients quickly on a single unit with dedicated staff; they shortened their hours, increased efficiencies, and enhanced outcomes.

The practice prospered, and so did we!

Urgent care drives census

Admissions were at a standstill in this general hospital without an Emergency Department. The Emergency Department is a feeder, and without one, we were not being fed. We opened an Urgent Care Center with coverage 14 hours a day; we could see patients within 15 minutes of their arrival, provide care, and transition them either to inpatient care or clinic follow-up.

At an El Paso facility, we were losing big dollars, and no one seemed able or willing to turn it around. Taking the job allowed me to (a) be a hero, (b) create a success story, and (c) position myself for advancement. By visiting the city hospital with the largest emergency room, we secured permission to discuss our situation with the local emergency physician group. While we could not offer competitive rates, we did provide an additional revenue stream and a less intensive workload. We opened a small unit that was open 8:00 a.m. until midnight seven days weekly. We promoted our service on TV and on billboards (there was no such thing as social media at the time), and we saw patients within 15 minutes of entry, or care was 'free.' Within a few months, we were so busy that we grew our admission rate by 40 patients per month, and we expanded our site, physician offering, and capacity. Eventually, we were open 24/7/365, and we had turned a loss into a profit center.

Accounts payable... the utilities

As a financial turnaround expert, my attention and talents turned to a 500-bed hospital that was losing $60 million annually. That was quite a shortfall, and we could not pay our bills, including the basics of electricity, water, and supplies. We owed the local gas company over $2 million; it threatened to shut us off, but because of the potential for negative media exposure, it chose to keep us operational. The negotiations were intense and resulted in a compromise that could be construed as an all-win: The hospital would not pay back expenses but would pay a monthly fee going forward that kept us fluid, providing the needed power, and allowing us to stay open. By getting paid monthly for future usage, the utility company got something — which is always better than nothing.

Whether you are negotiating within the workplace, or within the legal system, we all want the same thing, and that is an all-win.

PHYSICIAN CONSULTANTS

Doctors are sometimes hired as consultants. In this capacity, we recommend tracking your outcomes from baselines to demonstrate success and negotiate a percentage of incremental new revenues that you generate.

FAMILY

A family's dynamics continually change, and so family business and family dynamics are rarely harmonious. Think about the family setting, family-owned businesses, sibling rivalry, divorce, marriage, inheritance, death, housing — and the root of all evil might just be the color of money!

Perhaps that is why there are so many family business experts!

Having a family business raises the stakes and can complicate a family negotiation. Consider what makes it different:

1. The negotiation spaces

    - Most family members tend to be peace-keepers
    - They won't all come to the table
    - Some will be around forever (think forever family)

- Community sometimes matters
- Less involved in negotiation is not less involved in the outcome

2. It's not only about winning
   - The goal is creating mutual value
   - Loss is more than money
   - Outcome impacts future relationships/ families

3. Look at both sides of the equation
   - Listen, listen, and listen
   - Be willing to give a little to gain a little or more
   - Recognize that you do not know it all
   - Exchange authentic views
   - Identify and respect core values

4. Negotiate the bigger picture
   - Identify all the issues
   - Negotiate for the bigger picture, keeping those points in mind
   - Be aware of overlapping interests
   - Work cohesively to identify the most pressing issues

5. Make it about interest, not about position
   - Be transparent rather than fearful
   - Be patient and non-judgmental

It may be helpful to have a leader chosen from within the family, and that other family members become passive investors. Family members may have an equal say on important matters, for instance, but a consensus paradigm may be difficult to achieve. Perhaps that is why the field of Family Business Negotiator is growing.

LISTEN, LISTEN, AND LISTEN

Relationship	Key Factors
Relatives	- Long-standing or nuclear; emotional ties - Dependency - Loyalty - Sensitivity - Role delineation
Communication	- Complicated - Disruptive - Poor listeners - Judgmental - Perception/Reception
The Stakes are High	- Value of the business - Good for the family - Good for business - Multiple members and roles - Dividends

TRAVEL

Deals abound — every website, every airline, every hotel chain has an offer too good to pass up. As a business traveler, you anticipate business-class service and amenities.

Life goes on, and schedules change, flights are canceled, and we are inconvenienced. What does your preferred airline or carrier do when this happens to you? Be familiar with their policies, and know who will incur the loss.

Personal travel plans also change — due to weather, unusual circumstances, cancellations, and family matters. How you negotiate with the airline or hotel demonstrates how you settle in life.

Let me share an example. When writing to the head of a major airline recently about a change in plans due to weather and its failure to cancel a flight and therefore entitle me to a refund, I chose this as my email subject line: *"Why I Still Love AA."* You can be sure that this email resulted in an 'open.' That was my goal. The message addressed loyalty, and why, for more than 25 years, AA remained my airline of choice. In this way, the message addressed the recent challenge as well as the outcome (I remained a loyal customer), thus encouraging a favorable reply.

Within 24 hours, the response included an apology, a full refund of all costs, and a credit voucher.

It is about what you say and how you say it. We all write letters of complaint; in a high-school writing class, the teacher often provides examples of letters of complaint.

Have you ever complained?

We all have complaints about something; how we voice those complaints and how we negotiate for the all-win matters most. The airline in this example gained continued loyalty, and the customer obtained a full refund and more.

CULTURAL DIFFERENCES

We live in a multi-cultural society, and it enriches us. There are multiple sources of information on negotiating internationally. Companies such as International Orientation Resources (IOR) offer orientation for expatriates and their families, language skills, housing, and more.

We also sometimes rely on stereotypes — what we see in the media, profiling, and distorted expectations. By focusing on prototypes or cultural values, we can enhance the negotiation and create a win-all. How can you gain a greater understanding of cultural negotiations?

Consider these factors:

What to Know About Culture
Customs, beliefs, and values
Context
Background and behaviors
Who, what, where
Relationships
Possible barriers
Preferences and priorities

Working across cultures for the past 30 years required me to enhance my awareness of cultural differences and the effect on negotiations. Let me share an example.

Moscow

In 1992, with the dissolution of the former Soviet Union, newly independent countries were born. As the director of the Office of International Affairs for a hospital alliance, and subcontractor to the United States Agency for International Development (USAID), a non-governmental organization (NGO), the challenges were enormous.

My role was to manage multiple partnerships between U.S.-based hospitals and health systems and to negotiate a relationship with The Presidential Medical Center of the General Management Department of the Russian Federation when a prominent cardiologist pulled out.

Central Clinical Hospital (CCH)

CCH, the Presidential Medical Center's flagship facility — a 1,400-bed facility comprised of 10 clinical and four ancillary services buildings, as well as a (then) new birthing center — was exceptional by any standard.

Founded during the Stalin years, the hospital traced its routes to Moscow's typhoid epidemic of 1918 — when it was established to accommodate increasingly heavy patient loads. Following the events of 1991–1992, the hospital welcomed patients from a diverse selection of sources, including over 100 factories and businesses with which it contracted to provide employee care. A state-of-the-art Emergency Department, connected by a walkway to the International Patient Department, was constructed. Seven clinical areas of the first Corpus were renovated to Western standards based on the model developed in consort with Premier, Inc. The Center became a "foreign affiliate" of Premier in 1998.

U.S. government intervention and negotiation

In the summer of 1993, the Senior Medical Officer at the U.S. Embassy's Medical Unit in Moscow met with the General Director of the former Government Medical Center. The parties agreed to send a formal diplomatic note to the President and the Prime Minister asking that the Russian Federation Medical Center develop the capacity to serve the expatriate population. This letter included a rationale including interests regarding development and diplomatic requirements, and the desire to keep Russian monies in the country instead of having people seek their health care in Europe or elsewhere. The letter included: (a) a request by the Ambassador to establish a partnership program between the Medical Center and a U.S. healthcare system; (b) an agreement by the U.S. Embassy to assist the Russian Federation Medical Center in primary care, emergency care, basic internal medicine, orthopedics, pediatrics, obstetrics-gynecology, and other services.

A Russian national and physician at the Medical Unit was selected to assist with this process aimed at having the U.S. Embassy shift its business to the new clinic once operational and satisfactory. The General Director requested a Western-style patient care unit at both CCH and Polyclinic #1. He consulted with Premier, and an implementation plan was developed.

Memorandum of Understanding

A Memorandum of Understanding (MoU), detailing the working relationship between Premier and the Medical Center, was signed in Chicago on August 18, 1993. This event coincided with Premier's 10th Anniversary Celebration.

My legal department developed a management contract with the Russian Government Medical Center. A component of the management agreement called for the development of an American-style medical unit within CCH to meet the needs of the foreign business community. Concurrently, the U.S. Government gave CCH $4.7 million in medical equipment, including state-of-the-art surgical set-ups.

Partnership activities throughout 1993 to 1994 concentrated on training in primary care, diagnostic and interventional cardiology, nursing and medical education, quality assurance, insurance, obstetrics, immunology, hospital administration, cardiac rehabilitation, and Western medical care. Plans were developed for the renovation of a section of Polyclinic #1 and designation of the third floor of Corpus #1 at CCH as the International Patient Department.

Partnership extension

After the one-year USAID grant, the General Director approached the Ambassador requesting a one-year extension for $35,000 to cover the cost of partnership travel. A $35,000 grant was awarded, extending the partnership to April of 1995. Partnership activities were expanded to encompass rehabilitation and sanatoria management, high-risk neonatal care, marketing, and ambulatory care.

Under the direction of a Chicago-based architectural firm, plans for the renovated International Patient Department and Polyclinic were developed. Signatories to the construction contract were McHugh, the Medical Center; and Sharon Weinstein on behalf of Premier. The Medical Center committed $300,000 in funding to complete the renovations.

Construction at the hospital began on January 20, 1996, with the entire department shutting down. During construction, staff were given English language lessons and comprehensive instruction in the care and management of Western patients. McHugh International completed renovations on April 1, 1996, and the departmental Grand Opening was held for the public on April 2, 1996.

The result was a Western-style department with English-speaking staff, all of whom received training in the practice of U.S. healthcare delivery and customer service. A U.S.-licensed clinical nurse educator was on-staff at CCH for two and one-half years. A business/marketing manager was hired for one year. Premier's Moscow location employed a full-time administrative assistant/interpreter for nearly two years.

Accomplishments

Institutions involved in the partnership program have mobilized their resources to enhance the relationship between Premier and the Medical Center. Over 50 new affiliates have become involved in Premier's international initiatives. Business partners' level of participation in the initiative has been intensive, resulting in informal relationships between the Medical Center and Baxter International, Abbott Diagnostics, Johnson & Johnson, and 3M. Other firms involved in the program included Smith & Nephew, Kimberly-Clark, C. R. Bard, ECRI, Standard Textile, AMSCO, Becton Dickinson, Alaris Medical Systems, Hill-Rom, Ross Laboratories, ServiceMaster, Kraft Foods, McDonald's Corporation, and Hewlett-Packard. Premier personnel gained an appreciation for the knowledge, skills, and abilities of their foreign counterparts. Staff from CCH in Moscow shared a commitment to excellence and customer service. Significant accomplishments were made in the areas of nursing education and cardiology. By building on these achievements, the partners developed a program to support the Medical Center's expansion and quality goals for the future.

The negotiations were challenging due to culture, currency, the political climate, and perceived value. The partnership generated sustainable change, ongoing relationships, and mutual appreciation of the outcomes. This was an all-win that continues to give!

KIDS

We already addressed the un-sick sick child. Let's talk screen time and accessibility. Some families do, and other families don't — negotiate for screen time, that is! But, screen time is a source of stress.

Keeping kids offline from tablets, phones, and television can be a problem during vacation. But with teachers instructing students to use screen technology to complete assignments, it may seem like your kids are glued to devices from sunrise to sunset.

Teach kids to *do as you do* — model healthy behaviors that address on and off time. It's tough to get children to reduce their screen time if their parents are consistently on their phones, tablets, and computers. The more time that kids spend with screens, the less active they are. Implement a rule that there is no eating in front of screens.

What to Do	Why or Why Not
Lead by example	Limit your own time and attention to devices
Be the parent	Someone must be in charge
Be involved in their lives	Participate in school and after-school activities; listen to what they are saying
Monitor behavioral changes	Know your kids, their usual and unusual behaviors
Encourage other activities	Sports, outdoor activities, and creativity will always win
Impact of school	Many assignments are done using a tablet; schools are connected, and Wi-Fi exposure is said to be dangerous to long-term health

Negotiate, but remember to keep the following in mind:

For some families, screen time is unlimited, and that includes all devices. In other families, screen time is earned — available only on weekends except for homework — and safety precautions are in place.

Why does security matter and what are those precautions? A serious health threat that every parent should know about — Wi-Fi and cellular technology!

Is there an invisible danger — wireless radio high-frequency signals? Is it unsafe for students, and is it in your child's school or your own home? The impact on students' health is real and is manifested as headaches, eye strain, a feeling that something is in your eyes, dizziness, and increased heart rate. The symptoms appear at school and disappear once the child gets home, if there is no Wi-Fi at home, or if it is turned off when not in use! And cellular phones present similar challenges.

Let's look at Wi-Fi first

For parents, it is important to understand how especially vulnerable children are to electromagnetic fields (EMFs), as their nervous systems are still developing, and their skull bones are thinner than those of adults. Studies have now been done that show a correlation with these issues:

Behavioral problems. Children with both prenatal and postnatal cell phone exposure were 80 percent more likely to have emotional problems, conduct problems, hyperactivity, or problems with peers. Children who were only exposed prenatally had a higher likelihood of behavior problems compared to those who were only exposed postnatally, but not as high as those who were exposed at both times.

(Epidemiology July 2008, 19(4):523–529 and
Reuters July 29, 2008)

Autism and EMFs. The scientific community still debates the cause of autism, but a study conducted by Dr. Dietrich Klinghardt on autistic children and their mothers during pregnancy shows significant results, strongly suggesting that "electromagnetic radiation in the sleeping environment of the mothers during pregnancy, as well as electromagnetic radiation in the sleeping environment of children, may be key undiscovered contributing if not causative factors in neurological impairments in children, including autism..."

(http://earthcalm.com/lp-children-and-emfs/emfs-and-autism/)

So, let's look at the bigger picture, the real issues, and why screen time and connectivity should be negotiated.

Wi-Fi in schools

More and more schools have Wi-Fi throughout their buildings, meaning that kids are exposed all during their school day to the harmful radiation. Even when children are not actively using a computer, they are being bombarded with EMFs.

Wi-Fi in your home

At home, many live in the sea of microwave-range electromagnetic radiation created by the wireless router their parents have installed for everyone's convenience. Many kids have laptops with endless wireless connections.

Explore your situation!

So, are our kids being exposed to radiation? Are they increasingly sensitive to radiation? Based on studies related to cell phone tower exposure and increasing frequencies, many believe that Wi-Fi can have the same long-term effects as cellular phones — but both are hazardous to our kids' health. Think about it! Our children are spending the day under a Wi-Fi tower! In the past few years, Wi-Fi signals have been installed in schools throughout North America — probably in your community.

Let me provide an example of a current challenge. Many cities are installing *smart meters* which may violate safety limits on human exposure to microwave radiation. In some communities, they are being installed when residents have what is known as *electro-sensitivity*. There are also reports of smart meter interference with pacemakers and other implants. Two Naperville, Illinois mothers were arrested after they tried to block utility workers from installing smart meters in their yards.

Residents in many communities oppose the wireless smart meters, citing concerns about possible health problems that might be caused by the meters' wireless signal, which is always on. They have said studies show the radiofrequency (RF) signal could be dangerous, when combined with other RF frequencies already in existence.

Does that describe your community?

Should you be concerned? Yes! Should you be proactive in limiting and negotiating exposure for your children — of course, yes.

We have increased awareness — now, what can we do?

- Limit use of connected devices
- Limit your kids' exposure to Wi-Fi
- Use a Bluetooth
- Be aware of manufacturers' warnings
- Negotiate screen time

Consider a contract with your child to define the terms of use, an understanding of violations, and consequences. Many templates are available online.

We have the knowledge, and we are aware; let's *prepare for the negotiation.*

CHAPTER 6

PREPARING FOR NEGOTIATION

LEGAL NEGOTIATION

Whether your negotiation is a for a legal matter or in a commercial setting, the goal should be the same — and that is a scenario where everyone gets something, even if no one gets everything — a *win-win* situation. Whether that result can be achieved depends on two fundamental components of any negotiation — leverage, and relationships.

In some law school negotiations classes, you learn that the best result is a win-win scenario. The professor would present a situation, and the students would negotiate a dispute with a partner;

your grade was highest if both parties won. If one party was a clear victor, and the other was a clear loser, you would receive a lower grade. Both sides needed to feel as if they got something, even if they did not feel as if they got everything.

But in practice, there may be such an imbalance in leverage that it is harder to achieve that ideal result. That's because leverage comes from the ability to *walk away*, and the parties in a legal dispute may not be equally willing or able to do that. That's especially true when you are negotiating with the government.

If you are negotiating with the government in a criminal case, for example, the prosecutor typically holds all the cards. That's because, assuming the government has the evidence to back up its charges, the consequences of not making a deal are nearly always worse for the defendant than for the government. If the defendant turns down a plea agreement, the consequences are a risk of greater punishment. For an individual, that means a much longer prison sentence. For a company, that means a much higher financial penalty and the existential harm that may arise from being indicted in the first place. But for the prosecutor, the consequences are only being forced to present the evidence to a jury at trial. So, prosecutors are nearly always more willing and able to walk away from negotiations than the other party.

Indeed, the prosecutors who are the best negotiators are the ones with reputations for being good trial lawyers, because the defense lawyer knows that the attorney is perfectly willing to walk away from the negotiating table and go to trial. On the other hand, prosecutors with a reputation for seeking to avoid trials are less efficient negotiators, because defense lawyers know that those prosecutors are not as willing to walk away. The same principle applies if you are negotiating with the government on a civil or regulatory matter. If the private party is not equally able to walk away, then the government negotiator has superior leverage and can extract greater concessions.

As a practical matter, in this type of negotiation, the goal is not truly the *win-win* you are taught to seek in the classroom. While the government, of course, should find a fair resolution, its primary goal is to achieve the greatest possible penalty or sanction. And the purpose of the defendant or other private party is just the opposite.

This imbalance in leverage and these asymmetrical goals mean that it is not possible to achieve a true win-win in these circumstances. But that doesn't mean there is no room to negotiate and no ability to reach meaningful concessions from the government. That's because of the other fundamental component of any negotiation — relationships. The less leverage you have, the more your relationships — your skills at dealing with people — matter.

Your level of professionalism, your credibility, and your ability to connect with people are critical to any negotiation. But when you don't have a lot of leverage, they are your greatest — perhaps your only — currency. When you deal respectfully with others, and when people know that you mean what you say, your counterparts will take you seriously, listen to what you say, and perhaps be more willing to reach a fairer outcome. Negotiations are based on trust. Regardless of culture, language, or background, it is essential to establish a trusting relationship with those with whom you are negotiating. Negotiations may be between large institutions, but they ultimately are conducted by human beings, and so the ability to understand human nature and to influence people will be critical to a successful outcome.

Consider these key points in a legal negotiation:

- Know the facts and what the evidence shows
- Know the applicable law
- Know your client's exposure and risk tolerance

SPORTS

We know that sports teams have salary caps, and players are sometimes traded because the team has already capped out.

Let's face it, athletes often have extensive packages, and these packages are negotiated by experts in the field. They come to the table prepared, with data, and with a plan.

Sports contracts vary with the type of sport. Some are more lucrative than others, and to the public, seeing those numbers is astonishing. The career span is short, however, and the numbers on the front end must be high. Injuries can shorten the career span; players are in competition for their positions because farm clubs and those in the wings are eager to join the team. The tension is high, the risks are significant, the contracts are lucrative, and the games go on.

It is time to expand our thought process and consider *strategies* in real estate, academia, and even marriage.

Are you ready?

CHAPTER 7
STRATEGIES

Think about the strategies that you have used every day!

REAL ESTATE

We negotiated a lease, our very first, two years prior, and it was now time for renewal. We received an email notification that the rent would increase by $500 per month, 25% more than we were currently paying. How did we respond? Because we were under new management, and because we did not like the tone of the email, we explored our options, looking at properties in similar neighborhoods, and with comparable space and amenities. We identified several choices, and using an online service, we also identified the options within our complex. We wanted to work from a position of strength when we met with the leasing manager — and did we ever create power. We found that the apartment directly above our own, equal in square footage and amenities, was being offered at a rate $300 per month lower than our suggested renewal rate. We printed out the offer, and armed with that information and the comparison properties, we visited the sales manager.

We entered the negotiation in a positive way; we never criticized the current situation. We had recently written a positive review on Yelp about the facility, and they were aware of our report. We praised the building, the resources, the staff, and we stated how much we enjoyed being tenants. We also strategically placed our comps on the desk and suggested our top choices, both of which would force us to move. We told the agent what we liked about the sites, and we stressed the economics of the situation. To our surprise, she said that she would like to retain us as tenants and that she would personally research the circumstances leading to the increase in rent.

Less than 24 hours later, the increase was reduced from 25% to 2.5%, and we suggested a subsequent decrease in parking fees — bringing our future rental rate to that paid in 2015. We also negotiated a second-year lease increase of less than $50 monthly. Over a four-year period, our total rental increase is less than $50 per month — a win for us, and an all-win because the leasing company retained a valued client, did not have to prep the apartment again, and kept good faith.

ACADEMIA

Negotiating academic faculty workload

As with many universities, economic shifts and trends in higher education have led to greater demands on the faculty — an ever-increasing need to do more with less. Several years ago, we found that the administration was ignoring our requests to negotiate workload. It felt we were "just complaining." Communications nearly came to a halt. Administration's negative perception of faculty, emotions running hot, and the divided culture in the institution made negotiations extremely difficult. It was a challenge simply to get a seat at the table with the leadership team.

At this university, all degree programs are focused on areas related to social services, social justice, and community improvement. Faculty wrongly believed that just identifying the injustice of our situation would be convincing. A small group of us who had previously worked outside of academia argued that we needed to make the business case for our cause to incent administration to work with us. To address the problem, faculty formed a workgroup to find a strategy to negotiate for a lighter workload, and I led this group.

The aim was twofold: to compile as much data as possible to support our position that we were overworked and to convince the administration that it benefitted them to lighten our workload. First, we extensively surveyed all faculty members to determine what they did with their time. We gathered our benchmark data from comparable institutions regarding workload and salary, as well as policy and models for allocating workload among faculty.

It was a huge endeavor, especially given our overwhelmed workload status, and data were collected over a year's time. It was evident from the study that faculty were grossly overworked, each putting in an average of 60-70 hours per week — leaving little time to represent the university at community events, assist admissions with recruitment, or conduct scholarship to elevate the institution's reputation.

Our next step was to partner with our student government to survey students about their experiences. Students expressed that they felt faculty were unavailable and unhappy, and this impacted their experience. We also gathered reviews from recent graduates and investigated the reasons for our high student attrition rates across programs. Finally, we searched the literature for citations documenting the effect of negative student reviews on an institution's reputation and subsequent faculty workload.

Armed with data, we could explain exactly how the workload should be decreased and why it benefitted everyone. We approached the administration with a detailed, multi-year plan for reducing workload and a newly devised model for more equitable work allocation among faculty.

Our activities demonstrated that we were invested in our own and the institution's success and that we were not "just complaining," or waiting for someone else to solve our problem. We successfully negotiated to decrease the number of credit hours required for each faculty member and the cap for class sizes and to increase payments for teaching over a contract. Administration gained our investment in supporting admissions efforts and our willingness to work to enhance the institution's reputation. We left the negotiation with some *to-do's* that unfortunately fell to the wayside when a principal administrator left the organization.

We learned a great deal from the process; these are lessons that will guide future negotiation on an academic level.

What did we learn about negotiating in the university setting?

Make your case and do the legwork to determine how both parties will benefit

Negotiations cannot rely on the investment of certain people

> The loss of our champion in the administration meant we took several steps backward in our "to do's"

> Without a target strategy for implementing these additional requests, administration procrastinated and seemed to forget their agreement to collaborate in problem-solving

> And without using the negotiation conversation to develop a stronger relationship with administration overall, trust went with the individual who left

What next? From a personal and professional perspective, my goal will be to ensure that every issue is addressed. By coming to the table with data that informs and meets both my needs and those of the challenger, the outcome could, and should, result in an all-win.

MARRIAGE

We all know people who married their high school or grade school sweethearts — or perhaps they were neighbors, or maybe they met in college — and they have been together ever since.

We also know people who met, fell in love, and just *went* for it. Some of those marriages dissolved quickly, and some of them are still going strong after decades. If you know what you want, and the situation is an all-win, you can make it work.

Do you want to get married on, say, Wednesday? A key to negotiation is identifying your needs and going for it. That is the premise of this book and can be your premise in life. Ask for what you want!

How does that work? Sharon proposed to Steve on their fifth date and married him the next week. The first phone call closed the deal. He had a family, and she was searching for a home — more than a place to reside, but an actual home. So, knowing what she needed and wanted, she focused and said, "I'm not working on Wednesday, would you like to get married?"

And, we did!

How has it lasted? Long-distance travel, illness, working on the relationship, relocation, and negotiating for change have all been part of the equation. The rest is history!

The strategies worked — in the housing market, in a faculty setting, and in marriage. They worked because of *influence, position, and power.*

Now, let's discover those factors!

CHAPTER 8

INFLUENCE

WHO ARE THE INFLUENCERS IN YOUR NEIGHBORHOOD?

Malcolm Gladwell, in his compelling book, *The Tipping Point: How Little Things Can Make a Big Difference*, tells us that change is possible; people or social institutions can radically transform their behavior in the face of the right impetus. This is the ultimate *"tipping point,"* and the author provides examples of many forces coming together — many of them appearing small or inconsequential — that nevertheless result in large-scale change.

Social movements could have failed had they not had their own *salesmen* and *connectors*, the terms Gladwell uses to describe those with vast networks of people in various personal and professional pools who hear new ideas, talk about them, and share them. *Connectors* are folks like Bill Gates, Steve Jobs, and Sheryl Sandberg.

Because of their personalities and their ability to exist in numerous worlds and cultivate *weak ties* with a variety of individuals, these connectors make the world a smaller place by bringing people together. They perfectly illustrate the *six degrees of separation* theory.

Mavens are shoppers. It doesn't matter what the market is — cars, computers, clothes — the *maven* is the person with her finger on the pulse of the industry, the early adopter. Mavens accumulate knowledge about the industry; the maven is the guy in the cubicle next to yours who knows exactly what the next version of the iPod is going to look like and do. He's also the guy who has one first.

Salespeople are people who through the sheer persuasiveness of their personalities can sell ideas, products, and practices without even trying. We buy what they buy and do what they do because they make it seem so appealing, and we just want to be more like them.

Think of it this way:

Category	Responsibility
Connector	Knows lots of people
Maven	Takes the new thing being introduced, sifts through its real-world complexity, organizes, and translates it down to the simple relevant new bit
Salesman	Gets the recipient to take in that relevant new bit

They are the influencers because they have the power and the position!

POSITION

There is no doubt that position plays a key role in negotiations. Negotiations can and will be a power struggle. He or she with the most favorable position also holds the power.

Do you have power?

Factors involved in power include:

- Lack of dependence on others and BATNA
- Authority and control
- Psychology

Position is so much more than a title; it is also one's position on an issue. If a favorable issue with which most people agree, the position is better. If you are on the wrong end of a negotiation, your position is weakened.

Remember that one of you wants something that the other doesn't.

The essential question that neither party has asked the other is to explain the reason and motivation behind their position. The motivating forces are what we refer to as their negotiation interests or their *WHY*.

You can see why the steps outlined in *Preparing for Negotiation* were crucial to the conversation. Think about that section and the steps needed to negotiate successfully.

List your own key steps here:

1. _____

2. _____

3. _____

4. _____

Now, list them in order of relevance!

First _____

Second _____

Third _____

Fourth _____

What We Need to Know

The Issue	A clear understanding of the issue or problem
Obstacles	Similar and dissimilar potential obstacles to achieving closure
Separation	The ability to step back, when needed, to look at the bigger picture and to step away from (and out of) the issue
Negotiating Interests	Tangible needs or underlying components of the issue — payment, transportation, scheduling, and more
Problem Solving	Understand the problem and the obstacles to negotiate an outcome

POWER

Knowing the following rules of authority comes in handy when entering a negotiation. There are multiple sources with multiple suggestions.

One side does not have complete power	Even when you are at the mercy of a mortgage lender, you may decide to opt out
Power may be real or apparent	A final exam was administered in Eastern Europe. The policy there was to copy the answers from one another. We announced that we would adhere to U.S. standards; students were confused. Did we have a standard, or not, and did it matter to them?
Power exists only when it is accepted	If you don't try, you don't know. Consider the marriage example earlier in this book
Power relationships may vary from time to time	As the upper classman in school, you have the power – but that is middle school. Then, you enter high school, and again, you are the low man on the totem pole. Power changes throughout our lives
The side with the least to lose holds the most power	Consider the car example; you will, or will not, purchase that car. If you don't select one today, you may return tomorrow, visit another dealer, or decide not to buy but to lease. You have the least to lose, and therefore have the most power

How are you positioned when it comes to position and power?

If not you, then who has the power? Identify the influencers in your life, career, and future!

1. _____

2. _____

3. _____

Now, ask yourself the simple question, *"What if...?"*

CHAPTER 9

WHAT IF?

WE CANNOT REACH CONSENSUS

Equipment is needed in all work settings. Everyone wants to make a good deal on that equipment, including an extended warranty. Warranty in medical equipment is a challenge because technology changes rapidly.

In a medical equipment negotiation, we did not reach an agreement, and the sales representative knew that her senior manager had blown the deal; she respectfully asked permission to return with another team member and reopen the negotiation. Our second round resulted in an all-win. The hospital obtained a three-year warranty and would have settled for two.

When to call it quits

In all negotiations, you need to recognize when it is time to say, *that's it!*

As you now know, you must know your BAFTA. Follow these general rules for knowing when it is time to stop the negotiations:

- Observe: watch your body language and that of your proposed partner. Don't send confusing or conflicting messages.

- Consider the emotional climate: remember the section on personalities and the impact on the outcome. Be aware of the environment and how it makes you feel. If you are sluggish, fatigued, dehydrated, or just worn out, it may be time to call it a day. Consider what you can *live with* and if you are there!

- Pay attention to tactics: Be in the lead by directing the flow, the manner, and the ease of the process. You will be able to tell when the other party is uncomfortable, and you will certainly be aware of your comfort level.

From Voltaire, we learned, "A long dispute means both parties are wrong."

Could that be true? Knowing when and how to negotiate is one thing. It is an entirely different matter to know when to call it quits. Savvy business leaders recognize when it is time to call off the talks, break off the negotiations or the contract. Union leaders are familiar with the process; so too are sports agents.

There are times when one walks away for a cooling-off period, and there are times when it is just right to quit or to non-negotiate.

Those times might include:

- A body message signal from the other party that demonstrates avoidance
- When there is a *don't care* attitude among the parties
- When you see a molehill becoming the formidable mountain
- When BATNA (that best alternative) appears

There will come a time when your counterpart drives you away from the table. Playing hardball, avoiding the situation, yielding — will any of these strategies work, and do you want them to work now or ever?

There are disputes related to marriage, divorce, business closure, family matters and more that result in a *big chill*. Some of these negotiations keep parties from speaking, communicating, or interacting.

A pending arbitration may create pressure to delay the negotiation. A union representative may cede concessions unpopular to union members. The negotiations are stalled due to the big chill.

WHAT WOULD MAKE YOU WALK AWAY?

Think back to your past; list those things that made you walk away from a negotiation.

List those factors and how they made you feel:

1)

_____

2)

_____

3)

_____

4)

_____

5)

_____

Now, think about your future; what would make you walk away from a potential deal?

1)

_____

2)

_____

3)

_____

4)

_____

5)

_____

Remember that there is no point in negotiating with anyone when the viable alternative — calling it quits — can take you on another path.

Your goal is to get to the all-win! Is it possible?

Chapter 10

Getting to All-Win

Negotiation is a means of resolving differences between people. In the process of negotiation, we consider multiple factors. We've seen that throughout this book as we have shared stories and situations that crossed all lines.

WHAT NOW?

Ask the right questions. Are you satisfied? If not, why not? Do we want to pursue the process and continue to negotiate? If yes, what can we do to keep the negotiation moving along?

What next?

More importantly, what can we do to ensure satisfaction and that essential *all-win?*

You've seen examples of moving from conception to contact, from negotiation to an all-win. Consider the following stratagems that you might employ to ensure satisfaction, gain commitment, and maintain respect.

Focus on maintaining the relationship. Never allow the negotiation to destroy an interpersonal relationship; say something like, *"I see your point..."*

Focus on mutual interests rather than on opposing positions. Consider needs, desires, and fears. Parties at the table will often refuse to move from an important point.

Offer a variety of ways to get to all-win. There are so many ways to get to *yes*, even a partial yes. Consider emotions and choices.

Aim for an objective result that satisfies all parties. Find a result that is acceptable, independent, and that appears fair.

Now, list your three top negotiation strategies for getting to an all-win. What worked? What didn't work? If they didn't work, why didn't they work?

Top three strategies:

1)
_____

2)
_____

3)
_____

What worked?

What didn't?

If they didn't work, why didn't they work?

Can we close this deal?

CHAPTER 11

CLOSING THE DEAL

An individual should learn to compromise to his best possible extent. Remember that you cannot get *every*thing. For an all-win negotiation, *both* parties must win *some*thing.

TERMS, CONDITIONS, AND MORE

Perhaps you've been asked to sign a Terms of Use (TOU) agreement, which might relate to website or computer services. When you opt into a site to use its services, you may see this type of contract. We want to seal the deal, including conditions with which both parties are comfortable.

Tips for sealing (or closing) the deal include:

Opinions count. Consider saying, "In your opinion, will this approach solve your problem?" If the client says no, it is opinion and not fact; you can then address his/her concern in greater detail.

Asking for concessions. You have seen it with car sales: *"If I do that for you, will you take the car today?"* He wants the car off the lot!

Give something for nothing. A free value-add item can be helpful if handled correctly. For instance: *"I have an extra case for that phone today... if you take it now."*

Another appointment. You have an "emergency" call (that has been pre-scheduled at a certain time!) and so you need to leave — encouraging your counterpart to settle quickly.

Ask for objections. When you have completed the discovery process, and you are sure that your client understands your product or service, ask for any objections by stating, *"Is there any reason that we cannot proceed with your order now?"*

Direct close. This is a closed-end approach that allows you to seal the deal — today, now — and it works when you are confident, resourceful, and a great negotiator positioned for the all-win!

Our *survey* explored perceptions of successful and less-than-successful negotiations.

The results follow.

CHAPTER 12

WHAT THE SURVEY SAYS

SURVEY TIME

The best way to discover is to ask the question. We already know that to get what we want, we need to position ourselves with the knowledge, skills, and ability to negotiate. We also are good listeners.

With a passion for negotiation, and how others close the deal, the authors decided to survey a select group of C-suite executives, managers, and other professionals — and we listened! The study questionnaire was sent to a total of two hundred people, and the response was a sixty-two percent return.

The responses were consistent!

One hundred and twenty-four respondents offered the following picture of their best practices in negotiation:

1. What was your best negotiation?

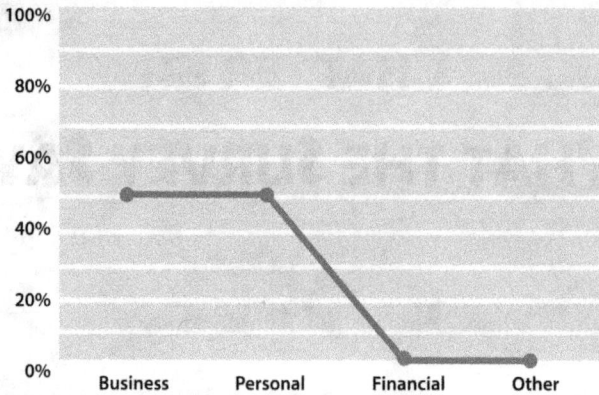

2. What was your opening strategy?

Responses varied from fulfilling an unmet need to wanting to create a win. Others wanted to build a relationship based on trust.

3. What role did you play in the negotiation?

CEO, HR Director, VP, Physician, Director, Customer, Client.

4. How did you determine what would be an all-win?

Active listening, identifying the need, mutual sharing and benefits, and having both parties in agreement and satisfied.

5. What was the outcome, and was it a success?

The answers stated, "Highly successful, both sides prospered."

---

6. What would LOSE mean to you?

Several individuals would have had to leave their jobs and start over. There would be feelings of discomfort, loss, and grief. Others stated that they learned from the experience.

7. What did WIN mean to you?

It created a path to generating infrastructure; a starting point for a long-term project. "It made me feel valued and cared for."

8. Who was involved on both sides of the negotiation?

Party 1	Party 2	Number
Medical center	Medical supplier	7
Public utility	Housing project	4
Physician	Billing company	8
Patient	Physician	6
Teacher	Union representative	13
Car salesman	Customer	7
Banker	Customer	2
Mortgage lender	Client	13
Real estate agent	Client	4
Grocery chain	Customer	6
Airline carrier	Frequent flyer	12
Dry cleaner	Customer	6
Supervisor	Employee	11
HR Director	Employee	3
HR Director	Manager	2
C-Suite	VP	2
VP	Direct report	1
Student	Teacher	7
Attorney	Client	4
Husband	Wife/Partner	2
Citizen	Government	3
Police officer	Victim	1

9. *Did the negotiation go according to plan? If yes, explain; if not, why not?*

"For the most part" was the typical response (over 55%). When the negotiation did not go according to plan, it was attributed to lack of preparation, failure to listen, failure to watch body language, and power struggles. When the negotiation did go according to plan, the success was attributed to strategy, preparation, listening, and knowledge.

10. *Were the parties involved multi-cultural?*

Responses included: Asian, and Eastern or Western European.

11. *Other than a workplace negotiation, what was your best family, relationship, or travel deal?*

A life partner topped the list.

SUMMARY

Consider these tips for mastering negotiations in your life, business, community, and family:

☛ Set your expectations and know your limits

☛ Use multiple techniques and tools to facilitate the process; know your counterpart and his/her expectations, wants, needs, and desires

☛ Recognize that you cannot always win. How many times did you run for elected office in elementary school, for instance, and lose because you forgot to vote for yourself, or because at that age, the boys vote for the girls, and the girls vote for each other

You may win, you may lose, and you may have success with an all-win outcome because you decided to *"Go for It... and Master the Negotiation."*

TEMPLATES

A variety of templates may be used to facilitate the negotiation process. We recommend these to prepare, to identify possible concessions, and to determine the relationships before and following the negotiation.

Preparing for Negotiation

Our Interests	Their Interests
1.	1.
2.	2.
3.	3.
4.	4.

Possible Concessions

Ours	Theirs
1.	1.
2.	2.
3.	3.

Relationships

Prior to the Negotiation	After the Negotiation
1.	1.
2.	2.
3.	3.

ABOUT THE AUTHORS

SHARON M. WEINSTEIN

With over three decades of global healthcare experience, speaking, training, and real-life, firsthand business experience, Sharon Weinstein negotiated her way into The Kremlin Hospital and convinced leadership to turn over a patient care unit so that she could create an International Department. Sharon is recognized globally for her ability to advance negotiations at all levels. Let's face it — negotiations are stressful!

She directed the Office of International Affairs for Premier, an 1,800-hospital alliance, for over ten years, and founded the International Leadership Institute. She holds the coveted Certified Speaking Professional (CSP) designation, the highest earned international recognition for professional speakers. This makes her among only 12% of all speakers to hold this designation and one of only 22 nurses in the world with this credential. The author of the award-winning *B Is for Balance, Second Edition: 12 Steps Toward a More Balanced Life at Home and at Work*, Weinstein's work has been shared with participants across the country and around the globe. Companies such as Premier, AIHA, Vistage, Sinai Hospital of Baltimore, Baptist Health System, Meritus Health, BD, Kaplan, YWCA, Kellogg Alumni, George Washington University Hospital, OR Managers, and BMO Harris Bank have partnered with

Sharon when they've wanted to negotiate for engagement, empowerment, and a *win-all* outcome.

She is an influencer!

STEPHEN M. WEINSTEIN

Stephen M. Weinstein left a lucrative career as a hospital Chief Executive Officer (CEO) to focus on wellness and prevention of amputations associated with diabetes. Weinstein was most recently with Doctors Community Healthcare, serving for five years as Chief Executive Officer of CommunityCare, the District of Columbia's healthcare system, comprised of Greater Southeast Community Hospital, Hadley Memorial Hospital, and DC General Emergency and Ambulatory Services. Also, Steve oversaw the DC Healthcare Alliance. Before coming to the DC area, Steve was President of Michael Reese Hospital and Cancer Treatment Centers of America, Chicago. His prior experience includes CEO positions at three Chicago-area community hospitals as well as executive positions with Chicago Osteopathic Health System, National Medical Enterprises, and American Medical International.

Steve is involved in professional, business, and healthcare industry organizations. He was named a Living Legend in Chicago and awarded the Rev. Martin Luther King Jr KEEPER OF THE DREAM AWARD by The Pastors Network. He served as a member of the board of both the Research and Education Foundation of Michael Reese Hospital and the District of Columbia Hospital Association. Weinstein studied at McGill University and received undergraduate degrees in economics and education from Loyola University, Montreal, Canada, and Florida Atlantic University, and a master's degree in healthcare administration from Trinity University, San Antonio, TX. As a senior principal consultant to Diabetes Amputation Prevention Specialists, he provides expertise in financial management, physician practice and clinic partnerships, and negotiations.

MORE BOOKS BY THE AUTHORS

SHARON M. WEINSTEIN

B Is for Balance Workbook: The Road to Stress Management

B Is for Balance, Second Edition: 12 Steps Toward a More Balanced Life at Home and at Work

B Is for Balance: a nurse's guide for enjoying life at work and at home

Developing Leaders for Developing Nations, In Feldman, H. *Educating Nurses for Leadership*

Memory Bank for IVs

Nursing without Borders: Values, Wisdom, Success Markers

Pharmacology, in Crudi, C. and Larkin, M., *Core Curriculum for Infusion Nursing*

Plumer's Principles & Practice of Infusion Therapy, 4th, 5th, 6th, 7th, 8th, and 9th editions

Plumer's Principles & Practice of Intravenous Therapy

Restructuring the Work Load: Methods and Models to Address the Nursing Shortage

Strategic Partnerships: Bridging the Collaboration Gap, in *Journal of Infusion Nursing,* September/October 2004

The Nurse's Handbook of Intravenous Medications

STEPHEN WEINSTEIN

Don't Sit on the Sidelines...Make MONEY Now: Strategies for Success

www.ingramcontent.com/pod-product-compliance
Lightning Source LLC
Chambersburg PA
CBHW072239290326
41934CB00008BB/1354